D1712567

THE ART OF
GLASS
PAINTING

Projects and artwork by Cheryl Owen
Written by Lisa Telford

TOP THAT!™

Copyright © 2004 Top That! Publishing plc
Top That! Publishing,
25031 W. Avenue Stanford,
Suite #60, Valencia
CA 91355
All rights reserved
www.topthatpublishing.com

Contents

An introduction to glass painting

Getting Started

The art of glass painting has historical roots, with many astounding
pieces on view in religious buildings and ancient houses around the
world. It is relatively easy to recreate these wonderful works of art in
your own home, or to give glass items a modern twist using the
same techniques. All you need are an eye for beautiful designs,
a steady hand, and the patience to practice the techniques
before attempting your own masterpiece!

EQUIPMENT FOR GLASS PAINTING

BEFORE YOU START

You may be wondering where to start with this seemingly complex hobby—but don't panic! The items provided with this kit are carefully chosen to allow you to start simply and work up to larger, more complex projects. This basic kit can be added to with inexpensive purchases from craft and hobby stores.

GLASS PAINTS

The most basic items you will need are, fairly obviously, glass paints. Colors can be mixed from the three prime colors (see page 8) but some colors are better purchased ready-mixed. Store-bought paints offer a wide variety of vibrant colors and allow you to choose exactly the right shade.

OUTLINER

The basic black outliner used in many projects is provided with this kit. It is used to keep the paints within a specific area of your work, although some projects avoid this for a different effect. Other colors of outliner can be bought, and metallic colors add an extra dimension to your work. They can be added on top of the paint when it is dry for an additional paint effect.

PAINT SURFACES

The paints provided can be used on a variety of surfaces. In addition to glass, they can be painted onto clear plastic, and transparency film (which can be bought in different thicknesses and sizes from office suppliers). If possible, test the paints on your surface to ensure that the surface will not corrode.

PAINTING TOOL

The tool provided is more suitable for painting onto glass than most brushes, and is easy to clean between colors. Read page 6 to find out how to use it to its best effect, and practice before attempting a project to get used to the feel of the painting tool and how it applies the paint.

CLEANING UP

As with most crafts, you should cover your clothes and your work surface before you begin, to avoid unnecessary cleaning up. Paint spills can be removed from work surfaces with paper towels and a small amount of turpentine; wipe up any excess and dab the stain before it dries. Keep the rim of your paint pots clean to prevent the lids sticking when they are stored.

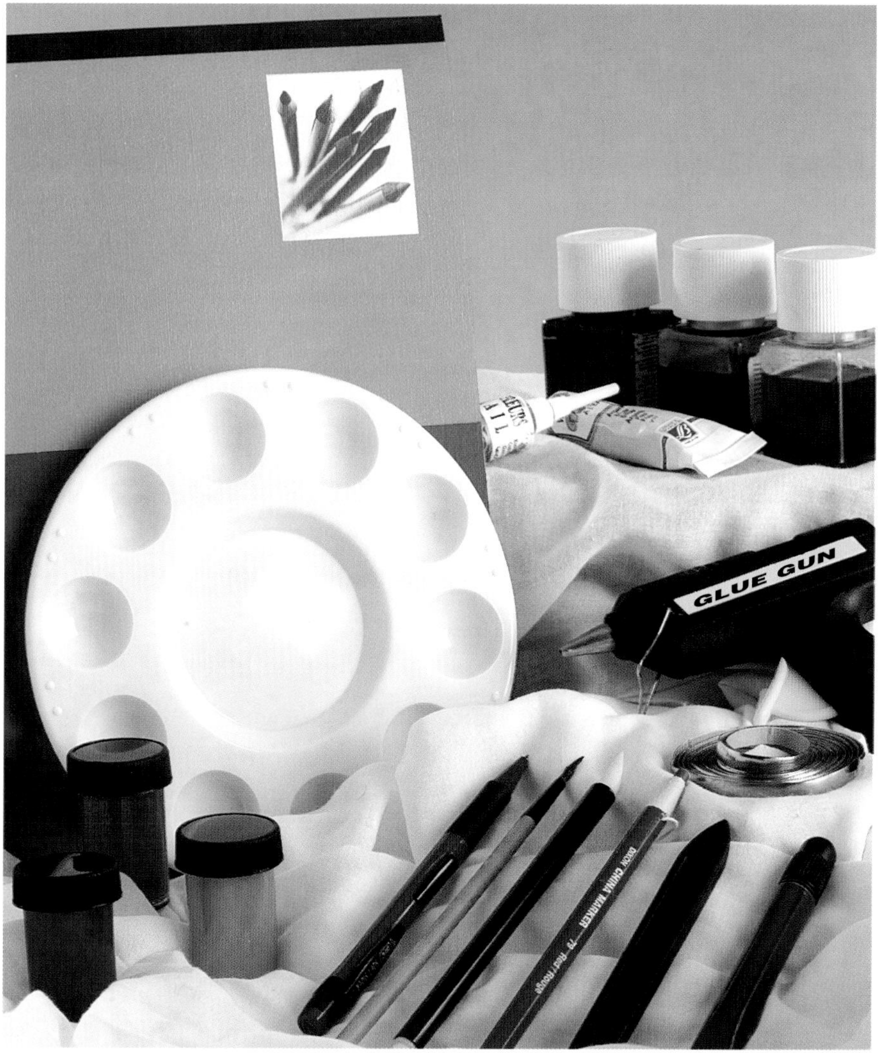
GLUE GUN
DIXON CHINA MARKER
79 Red / Rouge

Basic Techniques

Practice First

Like all new skills, you should expect to have some poor attempts before you produce anything of quality. Collect old glass jars to practice on, or buy inexpensive transparency film, which can still be used if your first designs leave something to be desired!

Applying the Paint

Dip the pointed end of the tool into the paint and dot it onto your glass surface. Practice spreading the paint across small areas without leaving "brush strokes" behind. Make sure that you have enough paint to fill the desired area; too little paint will leave more visible strokes.

Larger Areas

To fill larger areas of color, use the blunt end of the painting tool. Again, make sure that you keep adding additional paint as required to fill the space. Whenever possible, try to support your work so that you are painting onto a horizontal surface. This will prevent any color flooding to the bottom of the outlined area.

A Neat Finish

When the color fills the majority of the outlined space, use the pointed end of the painting tool to push the color right into the corners and edges of the area. If you have too much color, lift some off with the tool, or use a cotton bud to remove excess paint.

Changing Color

Always clean the painting tool before using it to apply a different color. Whenever possible, allow areas of one color to dry before starting work with the next color. Some projects use two colors merging into one another, and this should be done while the first color is still wet.

Techniques

Always start to paint in the center of a design, and work outwards as each color dries. Where colors merge, use a toothpick or the clean point of the tool to drag the colors into each other slightly. Some projects suggest applying a darker shade just outside your basic color for a shadow effect.

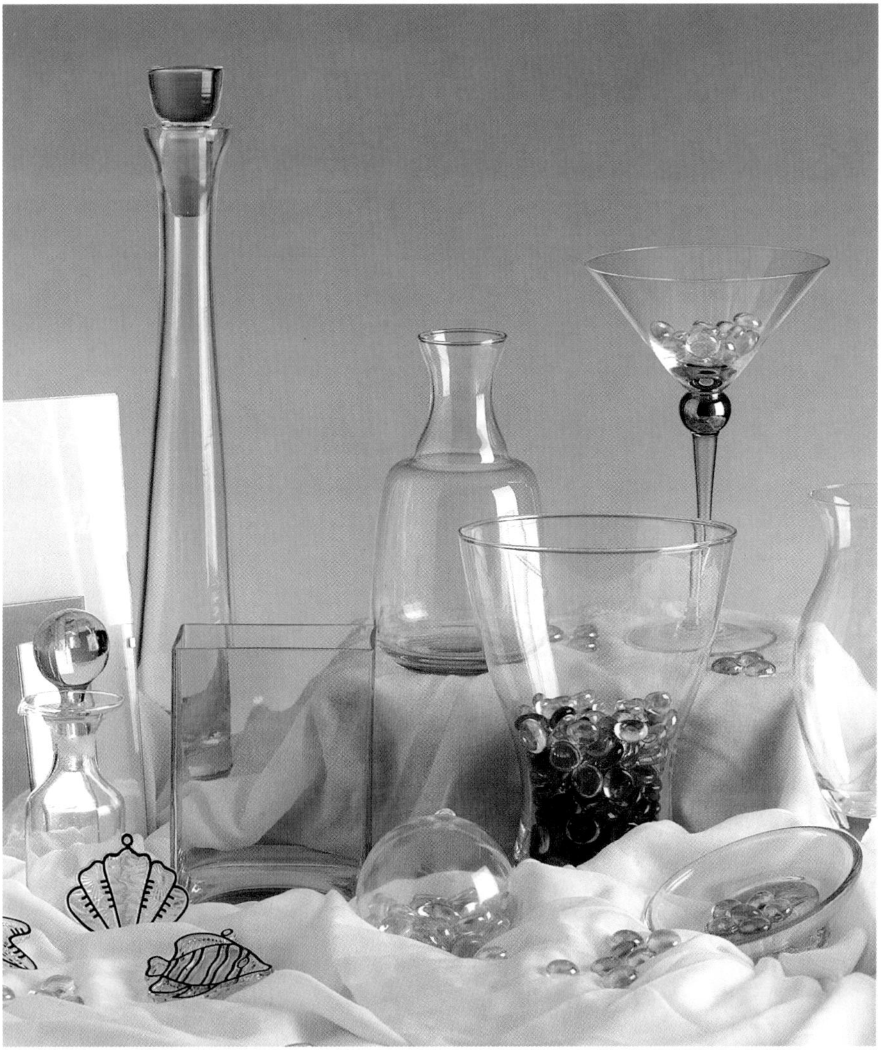

COLOR WHEEL

Primary

Tertiary

Tertiary

Secondary

Secondary

Tertiary

Tertiary

Secondary

Primary

Primary

Red + Blue = Purple
Yellow + Blue = Green
Red + Yellow = Orange
Red + Blue + Yellow = Brown
Red + Colorless = Pink

Colorless + any other color
= lighter shade of base color

Black + any other color
= darker shade of base color

Mixing Colors

Paint Palette

The basic color rules of paints also apply to glass paints: mix blue and yellow to create green, red and yellow to create orange, and blue and red to create purple. Experiment with smaller or larger amounts of each to obtain different shades and strengths of color. The color wheel opposite allows you to see easily the different shades available from the three primary colors.

Pastel Shades

To obtain paler shades of the three primary colors, and of the secondary colors mixed from them, you will have to add a colorless glass paint. This can be bought from hobby and craft stores, and simply lightens any other color when mixed together.

Ready-mixed colors

You will find as you mix your paints that some colors are more easily achieved than others. Certain colors will appear slightly "muddy," and it is easier to buy the exact shade you require to avoid this muddiness. Remember also that it is difficult to mix exactly the same shade twice; if you plan to paint an item over several days, or have large areas to fill with the same color, mixing your own paint could cause problems. A ready-mixed color will allow you to stop and start at your leisure without the worry of remixing the color to match.

GREEN

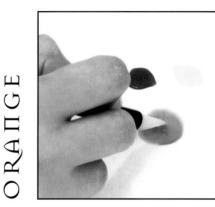

ORANGE

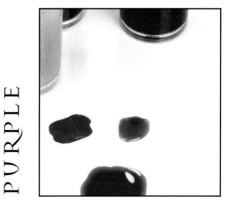

PURPLE

Applying Outliner

Using the Outliner Pen

The pen supplied with this kit has a pointed nozzle to direct the outliner in a fine, precise line. However, the hardest part of glass painting is to create a smooth, even outline without bubbles or blotches. Practice applying the outliner in one flowing movement—it really is harder than you might imagine!

Outlining Your Design

Most of the projects in this book use templates, which are all supplied at the back. Trace off the desired pattern and follow the instructions to position the template correctly. Once in place, you can simply follow the pattern with your outliner pen. Leave this to dry thoroughly before you start to apply colored paint.

The Finished Product

Many items you paint will be purely for decoration, but you should bear in mind what the item's use will be before you paint it. You should always paint the underside of any bowl or jug you may want to place food or drink in—never place food directly onto a glass-painted surface. Water-based glass paints can only be gently wiped clean, and never immersed in water for washing.

Solvent-based paints are more durable but painted items should still be washed gently and carefully, and never in a dishwasher.

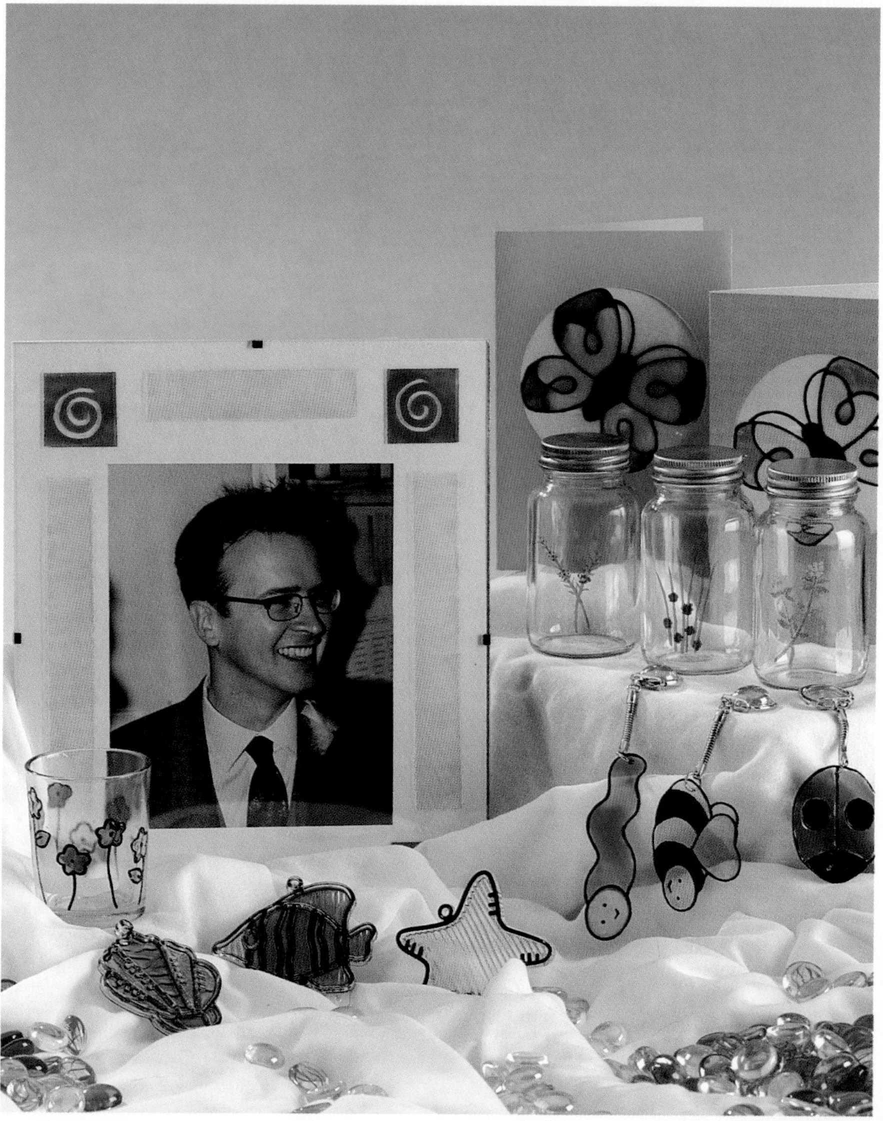

QUICK AND EASY PROJECTS

One of the most difficult parts of glass painting is successfully

applying the paint without leaving streaks and patchy areas.

Use these simple starter projects to perfect your technique,

before moving on to anything more ambitious.

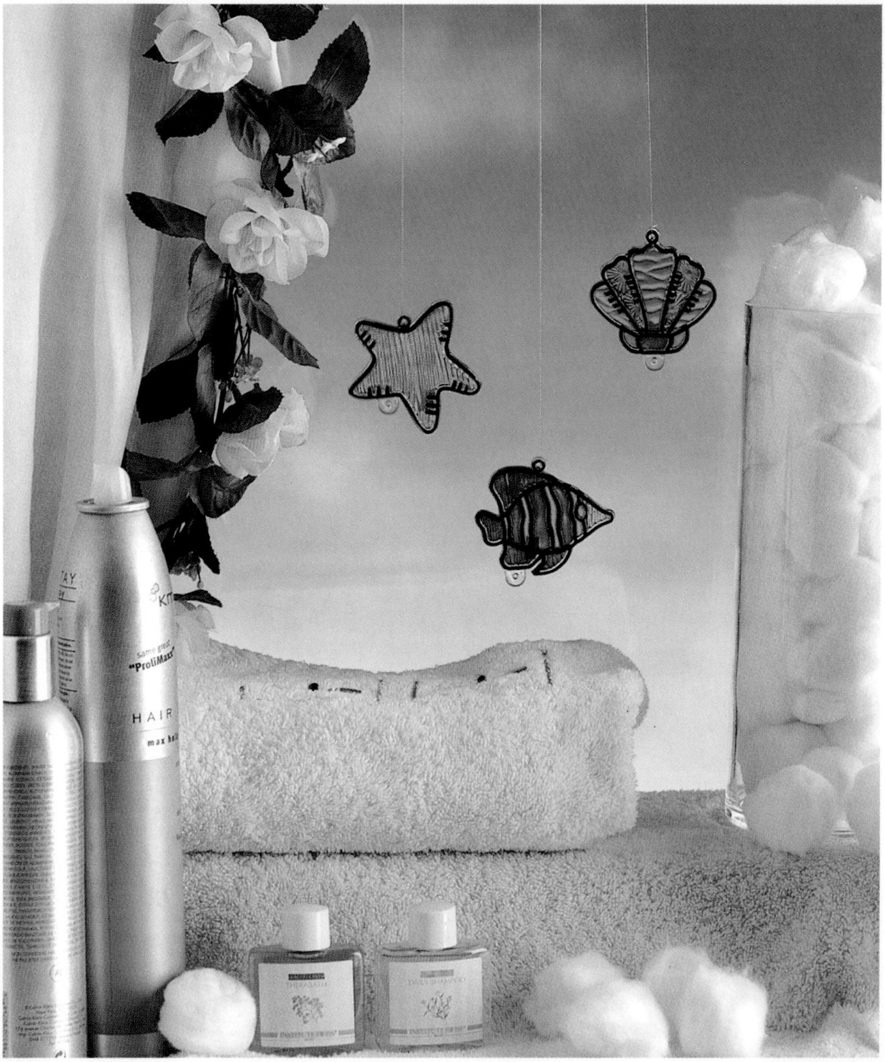

Sun Catchers

Red, yellow, and blue
glass paints
Painting tool
Three plastic
sun catcher shapes

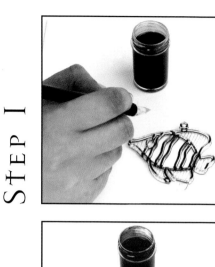

STEP I

STEP I Lay your sun catchers on your work area with the textured side of the ridged areas facing downwards. Work on the fish first, as it has very small areas which are good for practice. Use the pointed end of your painting tool to apply blue paint to the eye, the stripe across the eye, and alternate stripes thereafter.

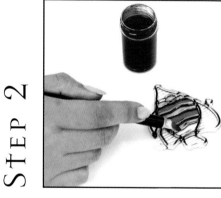

STEP 2

STEP 2 Now paint in the remaining stripes, using the red paint. Remember, it is easiest to start at the center of a piece and work outwards. Push the paint into the very edges of the area, turning the sun catcher to ensure that no areas remain unpainted. Paint the fins using the red paint, still working on the unridged side.

STEP 3

STEP 3 Finally, paint the head of the fish using yellow paint, and leave to dry. Paint the other sun catchers in the same way, working from the center outwards and applying paint to the unridged side of the plastic. Be especially careful to apply enough yellow paint to the large surface area of the starfish to avoid a patchy effect when it is held up to the light.

CLIP FRAME DECORATION

YOU WILL NEED

Glass clip frame
0.5 in. wide masking tape
Yellow and red glass paints
Painting tool
Paper towel
Cotton bud and turpentine

STEP 1   Remove the clips and lift the glass off the frame. Use masking tape to make a border around all four edges of the glass. Mask off a 1.5 in. square in each corner. Stick strips of masking tape 1 in. inside the outer tapes between the squares. Press the edges of the masking tape firmly to prevent paint from bleeding underneath.

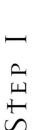

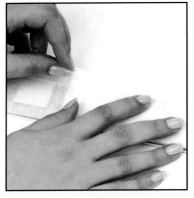

STEP 2   Paint each of the rectangles forming the border using a rich yellow color. Use the blunt end of the painting tool, generously loaded with paint.

Allow this color to dry. Mix a rich orange color to use in the corners. Paint one corner square, clean the painting tool and use the pointed end of the applicator to draw a spiral in the wet paint. Wipe off the excess paint on a paper towel.

STEP 3   Repeat this last process in each corner square, drawing a spiral in each while still wet. Leave to dry overnight. When the paint is completely dry, carefully peel off the masking tape. If necessary, neaten any edges with a cotton bud dipped in turpentine.

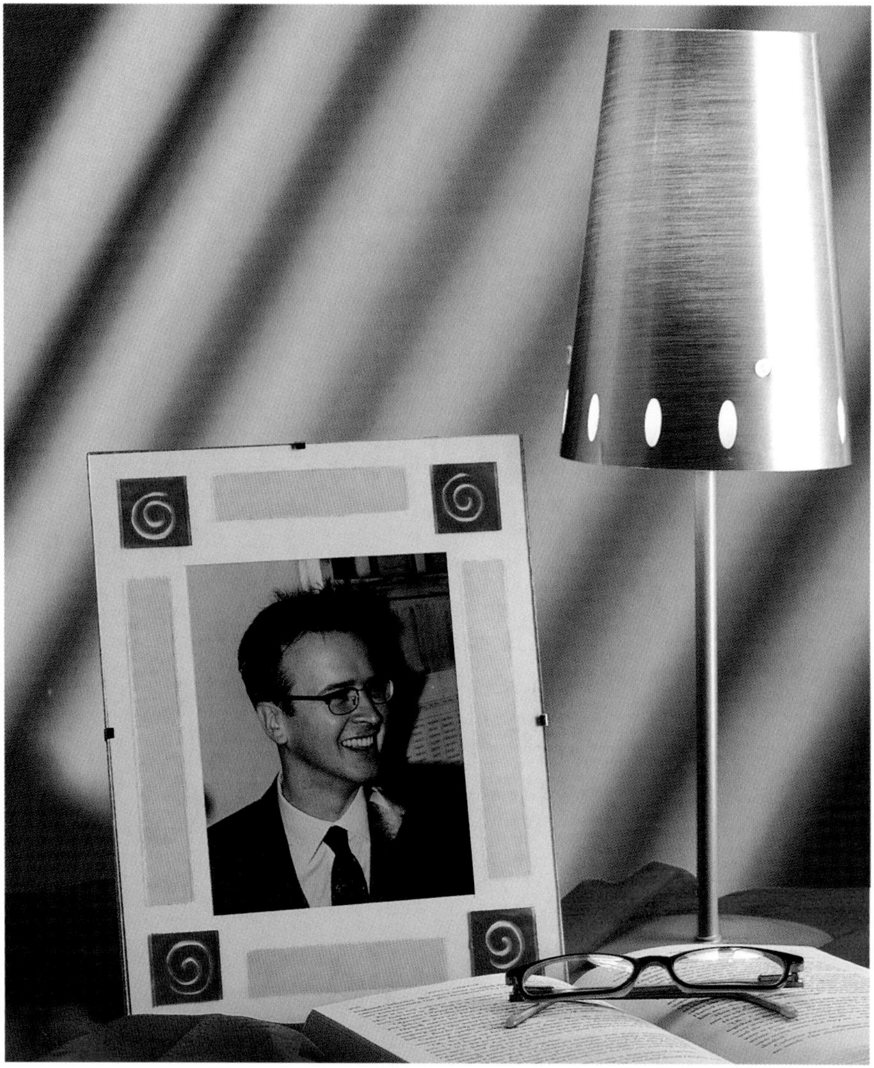

YOU WiLL NEED

Tracing paper
Soft pencil
Transparency film
Black outliner pen
Scissors

Glass paint
Painting tool
Pin or needle
Key chains

STEP 1   Trace the templates of the bee, caterpillar, and ladybug from pages 58 and 61. Tape the templates underneath a sheet of transparency film and draw around each outline with black outliner. Allow the outliner to dry.

STEP 2   Paint the black areas of the ladybug and the bee and leave them to dry thoroughly. Paint the ladybug's red back sections and dot in blue eyes. Paint the yellow stripes on the bee and paint the face in yellow as well.

STEP 3A   Mix together blue and yellow to make a green. Paint the body of the caterpillar with blue and green stripes, allowing the two colors to bleed together. Mix a little more blue into the green to make turquoise and apply around the edge of the caterpillar's face.

STEP 3B   Use this color to paint along the top edges of the bee's wings.

STEP 4   Fill the center of the bee's wings and the caterpillar's face with colorless paint. When all the paints are dry, cut out each shape. Pierce a hole in each and attach to metal key chains.

STEP 3A

STEP 3B

STEP 4

Nursery Mobile

YOU WILL NEED

Tracing paper
Soft pencil
Transparency film
Black outliner pen
Red, yellow and blue
glass paints
Colorless paint
Painting tool
Scissors
Mobile wires
Cotton thread
Superglue

STEP 1   Trace the sheep template from page 58, using a soft pencil and tracing paper. Tape this outline underneath a sheet of transparency film. Carefully draw around the sheep using the black outliner pen, omitting the cross. Repeat this to draw four sheep in total.

STEP 2   Mix four pastel shades of paint: lilac, blue, pink and orange. Use a different color for the hooves of each of the four sheep. Add colorless paint to each of the pastels, to make a lighter shade of each. Paint the wool with these new shades, matching each to the color of the hooves.

STEP 3   Add more colorless paint to lighten the colors further. Use these new colors to paint the legs, ears and face of each sheep. When all the paints are dry, carefully cut out.

STEP 4   To assemble the mobile, pierce a hole in each sheep where the cross is marked on the template, and tie thread through each hole. Tie the other end of each thread to your mobile wires. Cross the wires at the center and tie together. Dab the intersection with superglue to secure.

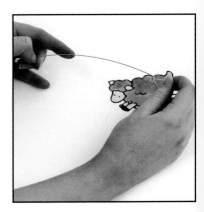

— HAnDMADE BUttERfLY CARDS —

YOU WiLL nEED

Tracing paper
Soft pencil
Transparency film
Black outliner pen
Scissors
Glass paint
Painting tool
Three fold window   White paper
card with 3 in.   Spray adhesive
circular hole   Double-sided tape

STEP 1   Trace the butterfly template from page 61 and tape the template under a sheet of transparency film. Draw the outline using black outliner, and leave to dry. Cut around the dotted lines of the template.

STEP 2   Paint the butterfly in your chosen colors, starting from the center and working outwards. Use the blunt end of the painting tool for larger, solid areas such as the body, ensuring that the paint coverage is even.

STEP 3A   Open the card and lay it with the left side facing upwards. Cut a piece of white paper which measures 0.25 in. less on all sides than the card front. Use spray adhesive to attach the paper to the left-hand flap of the card. Place double-sided tape around the edge of the circle.

STEP 3B   Stick the transparency film under the hole using double-sided tape. Attach the flap underneath the front of the card, using double-sided tape around the edges.

STEP 2

STEP 3A

STEP 3B

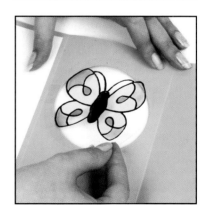

YOU WILL NEED

Tracing paper
Soft pencil
Scissors
Tea light holders
Masking tape
Black outliner pen
Blue, red, and
yellow glass paints
Painting tool
Modeling clay

STEP 1   Trace the flower template from page 58. Cut along the dotted lines, and position the tracing paper inside the tea light holder. Hold in place with masking tape. Carefully draw along the outlines with black outliner, keeping the line as fine as possible. When the first pattern is dry, turn the tea light and repeat, until you have outlines surrounding the tea light on all sides.

STEP 1

STEP 2   Paint each of the flowers in a simple primary color. Allow the flowers to dry before you turn the holder to continue, to avoid smudging the paint. Support the tea light holder between two small pieces of modeling clay or sticky putty to keep it in position.

STEP 2

STEP 3   Mix yellow and blue to create green for the leaves, and paint these on each flower. You could paint all the leaves at once, keeping the tea light holder vertical and turning it, but make sure that the paint doesn't run to the bottom of the leaf shapes.

STEP 3

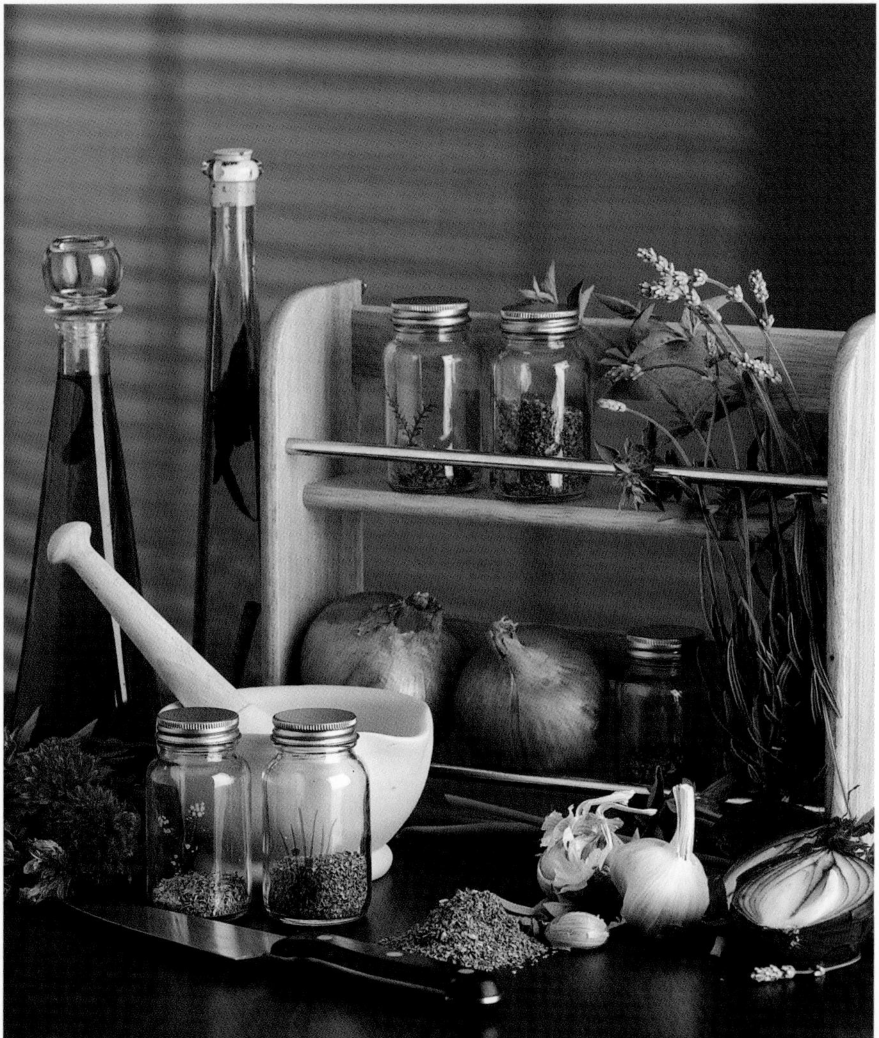

HERB JARS

YOU WILL NEED

Small glass jars with lids
Blue, red, yellow, and
colorless glass paints
Painting tool

STEP 1   Mix two shades of green
paint using a combination of blue, yellow, and
colorless paint. Paint the stems using careful
freehand strokes with the pointed end of the
painting tool or a fine brush. Add short
outward strokes to the rosemary stems. Paint
leaves on the thyme stems. Leave them to dry.

STEP 2   Add the flowers to the
stems of each of the different herbs. Use
pinpricks of blue for the rosemary flowers,
carefully dotting small amounts of paint in
clusters up each stem.

STEP 3   Mix a bright magenta pink
for the flowers of the chives. Form small dots of
petals for each flower. Add colorless paint to
this pink to make a paler pink for the thyme.
Form the main flowers at the top of each stem
with a cluster of dots, and add single dots
further down the stems.

STEP 1

STEP 2

STEP 3

Advanced Projects

As your confidence builds, it is satisfying to display your talents on larger, more complex projects which can be placed in more prominent areas of your home. Where possible, paint onto a horizontal surface before mounting your work on a wall or door, to prevent the paint running down to the bottom of the painting area.

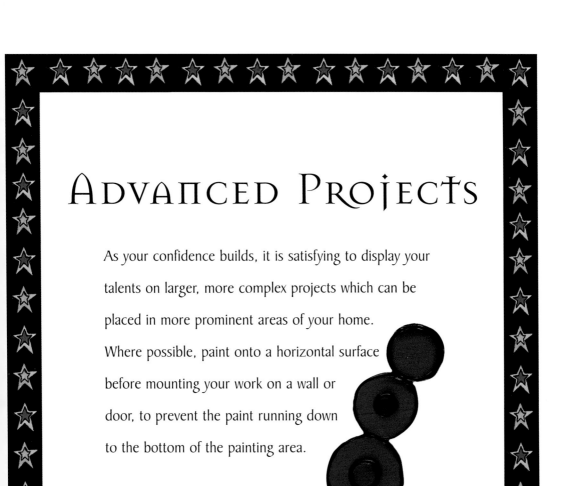

MIRROR PLAQUE I

YOU WILL NEED

Mirror tile (6 in. square)
Silver and gold outliner pen
Glass nuggets
Glue and China marker

STEP 1   Using the template from page 63, copy the design onto your mirror tile using a china marker. Draw the central diamond using the silver outliner pen. Use strong glue to fix a glass nugget in each corner of the tile, and leave them to dry.

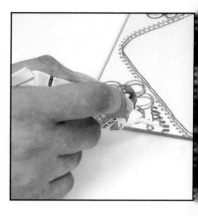

STEP 3

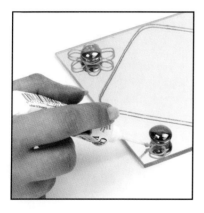

STEP 2

STEP 2   Draw in the flowers using gold outliner. Leave a margin of at least 0.1 in. between the petals and the silver diamond.

STEP 3   Add gold dots around the main silver diamond shape in the center. Draw a line of dots just inside the silver diamond, and another just outside. Leave this to dry, then decorate the remaining space in each corner using the silver outliner pen. Use freehand swirls and squiggles, keeping the lines fine and neat.

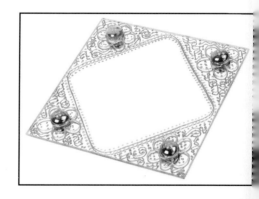

YOU WILL NEED

Mirror tile (6 in. square)
Black outliner pen
Blue, red, and yellow
glass paints
Painting tool
Tracing paper

STEP I   Cut out a 3 in. square of tracing paper. Tape the square to the center of your mirror tile and with black outliner draw around it. Leave to dry, then carefully remove the paper.

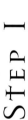

NOTE: When painting the plaque, remember the basic technique: start from the center and work out towards the edges. Push the color into every corner of each shape. Don't skimp on paint or the end result will be patchy and uneven. Paint the plaque in quarters, leaving each section to dry before starting the next.

STEP 2   Draw mosaic shapes, freehand, around the square. Run a line of outliner along each outer edge of the tile. It may be worth sketching a rough mosaic design onto paper first, to ensure that you're happy with the final shapes. Leave the tile to dry.

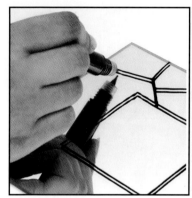

STEP 3   Paint each of the mosaic sections a different color. Again, it may be worth practicing your color scheme first on paper, to ensure that you don't end up with two adjacent sections of the same color. The finished plaque should have a balance of color overall.

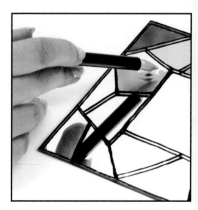

Aппiversary Bowl

YOU WiLL ПEED

Tracing paper
Soft pencil
Scissors
Shallow, wide-rimmed
glass bowl
Masking tape
Silver outliner pen
Blue, red, and yellow glass paints
Painting tool

STEP I   Trace the flower and leaf templates from pages 34 and 62 onto tracing paper. Carefully draw the monograms of your choice, (from page 62), onto the tracing paper.

STEP 2   Cut out the templates and position them under the rim of the bowl using small pieces of masking tape to secure them. Place the crossed leaves between the monograms with the single leaves at each side. Ensure that the flowers are evenly spaced around the rest of the bowl, with varying numbers of leaves.

STEP 3   Very carefully draw along the outline of each shape with silver outliner. Keep the lines as fine and delicate as possible, using a flowing movement for the spirals of each flower. Leave the outliner to dry, overnight if possible.

STEP I

STEP 2

STEP 3

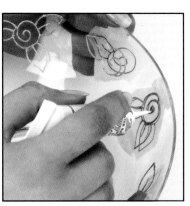

Step 4   Mix the paint for the roses, using a large amount of red with a small dab of yellow until you achieve the color you desire. Carefully paint in each of the flowers.

Step 4

Step 5   Add more yellow to the color of the flowers, and use this new color to paint in each of the monogrammed initials. Leave these colors to dry.

Step 5

Step 6   Finally, mix blue and yellow to make green for the leaves. Paint each of the leaves, working around the bowl, being careful not to smudge the previous paint as you turn the bowl around.

Step 6

Templates

SPOTTED VASE

YOU WILL NEED

Circular stickers—
two sizes
Glass vase
Ceramic tile or old plate
Natural sponge
Glass paint—colors of
your choice

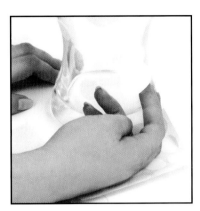

STEP 1

STEP 1   Stick the stickers to the vase to create a random pattern of spots. Make sure that the edges are pressed down firmly to prevent paint bleeding underneath when it is applied.

STEP 2   Mix your chosen color of paint on the tile or old plate. Use the sponge to dab at the paint and then apply the paint to the vase. You should be able to work around the whole vase in one session, as the paint is not applied liberally enough to run. Experiment with holding the vase upside down on one hand to apply the paint all over.

STEP 2

STEP 3   When the paint is completely dry, remove the stickers to reveal the pattern of spots.

STEP 3

Celtic Carafe and Glasses

YOU WILL NEED

Tracing paper
Soft pencil
Scissors
Water carafe and glasses
Masking tape
China marker
Gold outliner pen
Blue and yellow glass paints
Painting tool
Modeling clay or sticky putty

TEMPLATES

STEP 1   Trace both Celtic templates and cut them out carefully. Tape the large template to the front of the carafe with small pieces of masking tape. Draw around the edge with a china marker, and then remove the template.

STEP 1

STEP 2   Draw over the china marker lines with gold outliner. Also follow the lines which form the intersections of the pattern with gold outliner. Copy the template exactly to get the intersections in the correct places. Leave the outliner to dry completely.

STEP 2

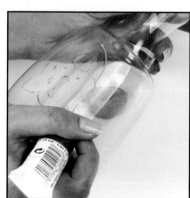

38

STEP 3A Mix a good supply of a shade of green that you're happy with. Separate part of this and add a touch of red to darken the green. Alternatively, you could use a ready-made green and add a little black paint to get a darker shade.

STEP 3B Support the carafe on its side, using modeling clay or sticky putty to keep it in position. Apply a little dark green paint to the intersection of one section. Fill the rest of the section with light green paint and blend the two together.

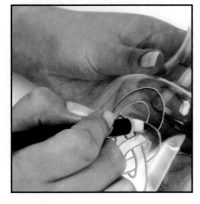

STEP 4 Paint all the sections of the carafe in the same way. Leave the carafe to dry in a horizontal position to prevent the paint from running.

STEP 5 Tape the small Celtic motif to the inside of the glass. Use the gold outliner to draw a line around the outline, and leave it to dry.

STEP 6 Paint the motif on the glass in the same way you painted the motif on the carafe, using a small amount of dark green paint at the intersecting points, and paler green for the main parts of each section. Leave to dry.

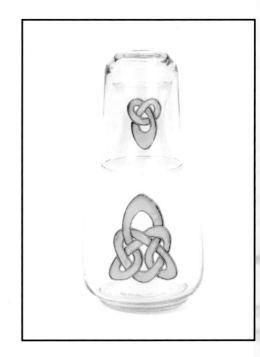

YOU WILL NEED

Tracing paper
Soft pencil
Straight-sided
glass bowl
Pitcher
Scissors
Masking tape
Glass paint—colors of your choice
Painting tool
Silver outliner pen

STEP 1   Trace the flower template from page 42. Repeat enough times to fit around the edge of your bowl. Roughly cut out these templates and use masking tape to hold them in position all around the bowl.

STEP 2   Support the bowl on its side so that you will be painting the flowers horizontally. Position one flower on top. Paint this first flower violet. Leave it to dry before turning the bowl to paint the next flower blue. Again, leave this to dry before turning the bowl to paint the next flower. Paint this one a mixture of violet and blue blended together.

STEP I

STEP 2

Salad Bowl & Pitcher

Step 3

STEP 3   Continue painting the flowers, alternating the colors between violet, blue and violet/blue mixed. When the final flower is dry, stand the dish on its base. Use a silver outliner pen to add tiny dots to the center of each flower. Remove the tracings from inside the bowl.

STEP 4   To paint the pitcher, tape a single flower template inside, in the position you want it. Paint over the flower in your favorite color. When the flower is dry, add silver dots in the center to match the bowl.

Step 4

Template

Art Deco Door Panel

YOU WILL NEED

Tracing paper
Soft pencil
Masking tape
Black outliner pen
Glass paint—
colors of your choice
Painting tool

STEP 1   Trace the Art Deco design from page 59. You may need to enlarge the template on a copier to fit the door panel you intend to paint. When the template is the correct size, trace it onto tracing paper. If at all possible, remove the panel to paint it in a horizontal position.

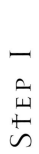

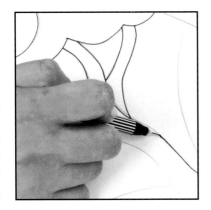

STEP 2   Tape the template behind the glass panel. Draw along each of the outlines with black outliner. Try to use long, flowing movements for each of the lines, keeping each line approximately the same thickness. Leave overnight to ensure the outline is completely dry.

STEP 3   Paint the trunk of the tree first, as it is the central part of the design. If you are painting the panel in position, you may find that you have to keep removing paint that has sunk to the bottom of the section, and reapplying paint at the top of the section, to ensure an even color all the way down. When the trunk is dry, begin to paint the blue of the sky, starting in the center.

STEP 3

STEP 4   Paint each of the dark green sections of the tree's leaves. Allow these to dry, and then paint the pale green sections. At the same time, paint the pale green undergrowth sections. Let these dry completely.

STEP 4

STEP 5   Paint the large yellow areas at each side of the tree trunk. When these are dry, paint the orange sections alongside.

STEP 5

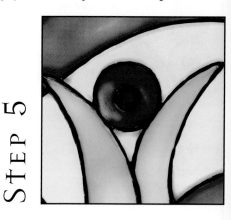

STEP 6   Finally, paint in the brightly colored flowers. Start at the center of each and fill in the outer petals afterward.

STEP 6

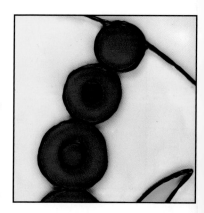

LEADED VASE

YOU WILL NEED

Straight-sided glass vase
Lead stripping (0.25 in. wide)
Craft knife/scissors
Glass paint—colors of your choice
Boning peg
Painting tool
Paper towel

STEP I Lead stripping can be bought from most craft stores, and should have its own instructions for use. The type used in this project has a self-adhesive back, and should be used with a boning peg to help it adhere to the glassware. Use scissors or a craft knife to cut the strips to the correct length.

STEP I

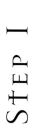
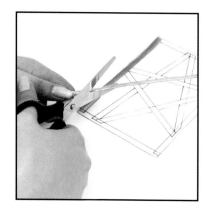

STEP 2A Refer to the template on page 60 to stick the lead stripping in an asymmetric star shape, on the front of the vase. Cut the strips to the correct length, leaving the ends 0.1 in. inside the edges of the glass.

STEP 2A

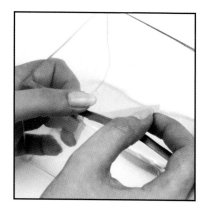

STEP 2B Fix the strips firmly in place using a boning peg, and following the manufacturer's instructions.

STEP 2B

STEP 3   Fasten a piece of lead stripping down each outside edge of the front panel, again leaving the strips 0.1 in. short at the top and bottom. Stick a strip of leading right around the top of the vase, overlapping the edges at the back. Repeat at the bottom of the vase. Check all around to ensure that the edges are hidden and all strips are stuck firmly.

STEP 4   Lie the vase on its back with the leaded side facing upwards. Paint the center section of the star. Use the pointed end of your painting tool to remove circles of paint to reveal the glass underneath. Wipe the excess paint off the tool onto the paper towel.

STEP 4

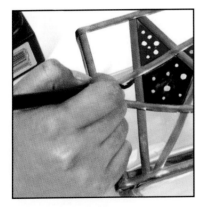

STEP 5   Paint each point of the star, one by one. Before painting the next point, use your painting tool to remove circles of paint. Wipe the tool clean on the paper towel and then move on to paint the next point.

STEP 5

STEP 6   Paint one section of the background area using blue paint. Use the pointed end of your painting tool to remove waves of paint, wiping the tool clean each time. Allow the first section to dry and repeat with each of the other background sections.

STEP 6

WALL LIGHT

YOU WILL NEED

Tracing paper
Soft pencil and
a harder pencil
Scissors
Masking tape
Wall light
Black outliner pen
Glass paint—
colors of your choice
Painting tool

STEP 1   Trace the template from page 55 onto ordinary paper. Use a copier to enlarge it to the size you need for your wall light, and then trace it onto tracing paper.

STEP 2   Draw over the design on the reverse using a very soft pencil. Roughly cut out the template.

STEP 3   Make cuts into the template to allow you to fit it around the curve of the light. Tape it in place, and draw over the lines with a sharp, hard pencil to transfer the design onto the glass. Remove the template.

STEP 1

STEP 2

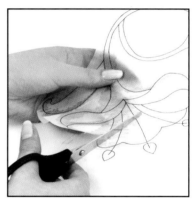

STEP 3

STEP 4   Carefully draw all the lines of the design using black outliner. Always try to work from the top downwards, to avoid smudging the lines. Leave the outline to dry, overnight if possible.

STEP 4

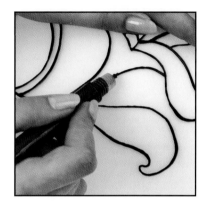

STEP 5   Paint the main flower part of the design, using red for the petals. Start from the center petal and work outwards. Add depth to the base of some petals by applying a darker shade at the bottom, and a lighter color at the top. Blend these colors together, and leave to dry.

STEP 5

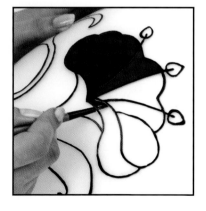

STEP 6   Paint the stamens orange. Turn the light, supporting it so that you can paint the left side in a flat position. Paint the different shades of green, blending them together. Leave this to dry.

STEP 6

STEP 7   Turn the light onto its other side so that you can paint the remaining green sections in a flat position. Leave these to dry before fixing the light to the wall.

STEP 7

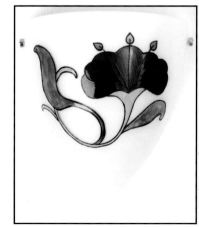

TEMPLATE

CHRISTMAS BAUBLES

YOU WILL NEED

Tracing paper
Soft pencil
Scissors
Two-part clear plastic baubles
Black outliner pen
Glass paint—colors of your choice
Painting tool

STEP 1   Trace the Christmas templates from page 60 onto tracing paper. Cut them out roughly and make slits in the sides so that the template will fit inside the concave shape of the bauble. Separate the two bauble halves and tape the template inside one.

STEP 2   Draw around the shapes with black outliner, carefully supporting the underneath of your bauble, with your hand. When the outliner is dry, paint the green of the Christmas tree. Move the bauble to keep the painted area horizontal, to prevent the paint from accumulating in one area.

STEP 3   When the paint is dry, continue painting in the central areas of the other designs. Leave them to dry, then reassemble the parts of the baubles before hanging them.

NOTE: If you cannot buy two-part baubles, cut out each template carefully and tape each to the front of a bauble. Draw around the designs with a china marker before going over these lines with outliner.

STEP 1

STEP 2

STEP 3

TEMPLATES

TEA LIGHT HOLDER PAGE 24-25

NURSERY MOBILE PAGE 20-21

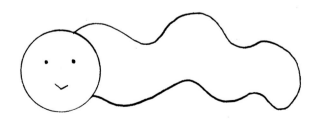

KEY CHAIN PAGE 18-19

Templates

CHRISTMAS BAUBLES 56-57

Templates

BUTTERFLY CARDS PAGE 22-23

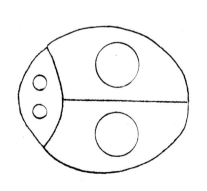

KEY CHAINS PAGE 18-19

Templates

MIRROR TILE PAGE 30

Congratulations!

Now You Can Paint Glass

Hopefully, you now feel confident in your abilities, and are bursting with ideas for other glass items to paint. Keep looking for new areas to work on; there may be glass or mirrored panels around your home which would benefit from an added touch of color. You can also find many bargain purchases at flea markets, charity events and yard sales—simple items will look extremely effective when you work your magic on them!